Thomas Sedgwick Steele

Paddle and portage, from Moosehead lake to the Aroostook river

Thomas Sedgwick Steele

Paddle and portage, from Moosehead lake to the Aroostook river

ISBN/EAN: 9783337156671

Printed in Europe, USA, Canada, Australia, Japan

Cover: Foto ©Andreas Hilbeck / pixelio.de

More available books at **www.hansebooks.com**

PADDLE AND PORTAGE,

FROM

MOOSEHEAD LAKE TO THE AROOSTOOK RIVER,

MAINE.

BY

THOMAS SEDGWICK STEELE,
AUTHOR OF "CANOE AND CAMERA," MAPS OF MAINE, ETC.,

> " Hunting is the noblest exercise,
> Makes men laborious, active, wise,
> Brings health, and doth the spirits delight,
> It helps the hearing and the sight;
> It teacheth arts that never slip
> The memory, good horsemanship,
> Search, sharpness, courage, and defence,
> And chaseth all ill habits thence."
>
> JONSON'S MASQUES.

WITH OVER SIXTY ILLUSTRATIONS,
AND MAP 20 x 30 INCHES OF THE CANOE COURSES OF NORTHERN MAINE.

BOSTON:
ESTES AND LAURIAT,
299–305 WASHINGTON STREET.
1882.

COPYRIGHT.
THOMAS SEDGWICK STEELE,
1882.

Lyman B. Goff,
of
Pawtucket, R. I.

Companion on this tour, with
whom I shared its pleasures and its
dangers, its discomforts and
its successes, this book
is affectionately
dedicated,
in token of my sincere regard
and friendship.

Hartford, Conn., 1882.   C. S. S.

CONTENTS.

CHAPTER I.

The start.—Unwarranted assumptions.—Our guides and outfit.—A flimsy wharf.—Railroading of the old days.—Contemptible deceit toward dumb animals.—Commencement of fun on the "Carries."—We go into camp.—First night in the wilds, ... Page 15

CHAPTER II.

Moving on.—Pine Stream Falls.—Chesuncook Lake and Farm.—Umbazookus Carry.—A dry ground sleighing party.—Further experience with the horse.—A glimpse of desolation.—Chamberlin Lake.—A vision.—Eagle Lake.—Smith Brook.—Haymoak Falls.—Trout Stories, ... Page 36

CHAPTER III.

In rough water.—North Twin Stream.—An Indian paddle for future use.—Breezes, blankets, cold and ice.—Spider Lake.—Manifold charms of camp life.—At work with the traps.—Concerning beaver.—We proclaim our intentions, ... Page 60

CHAPTER IV.

Osgood Carry.—The pack-horse league.—Novel trick in pedestrianism.—Camp on Echo Lake.—Hiram tells a story.—Sluicing a dam.—More concerning beaver.—Camp at the Mansungun Lakes, Page 79

CHAPTER V.

A vision on the lake.—Nichols' birch-horn.—A midnight hunt under a cold moon.—Calling the moose, ... Page 104

CHAPTER VI.

Decrease of our provisions.—Face to face with starvation.—Sore trials.—Shoeing canoes.—Through the storm.—We sight the waters of the Aroostook.—"Hurrah!" . . . . Page 115

CHAPTER VII.

Redeemed from starvation.—The first habitation on the Aroostook.—Mr. Botting's house.—The tourograph astonishes the natives.—Purchasing supplies at Masardis.—Homeward Bound.—*Au Revoir!*

Page 131

ILLUSTRATIONS.

1. SUNRISE ON ECHO LAKE,
2. DEDICATION,
3. A BEAVER DAM,
4. INITIAL "O,"—LEAVING MOOSEHEAD LAKE,
5. OUR GUIDES,
6. A SERIO-COMIC,
7. THE FIRST CAMP,
8. THE BEST MAN TO WIN,
9. NIGHT ON THE WEST BRANCH,
10. INITIAL "B,"
11. CHESUNCOOK LAKE,
12. CHESUNCOOK FARM,
13. UMBAZOOKUS STREAM,
14. PORTAGE,
15. OUTLET OF CHAMBERLIN LAKE,
16. CHAMBERLIN FARM,
17. FACETIÆ,
18. HAYMOAK FALLS,
19. GOOD SPORT,
20. THE DOG,

ILLUSTRATIONS.

21. INITIAL "E,"
22. A COLD WAVE,
23. LOW—THE POOR INDIAN,
24. DEVELOPING A PLATE,
25. "TREES PILED ON TREES,"
26. TWILIGHT IN THE WILDS,
27. EVACUATION,
28. "ON TO THE AROOSTOOK,"
29. INITIAL "I,"
30. THE PACK-HORSE LEAGUE,
31. AT NIGHT BY THE CAMP FIRE,
32. "BY DINT O' PUSHIN' AN' HAULIN'"—
33. "FOLLERIN' HIS SLOAT—HALLOO!"
34. "BEAT HIM LIKE AN OLD CARPET,"
35. "SAT ALL NIGHT WATCHIN' IT BURN DOWN,"
36. BEAVER DAM—FOUR FEET HIGH—ONE HUNDRED FEET WIDE,
37. SLUICING A DAM,
38. CHASE BROOK,
39. ODDS AND ENDS,
40. INITIAL "T,"
41. "MOOSE? YOU DON'T SAY SO!"
42. "OH, SUCH A PAIR OF HORNS!"
43. THE DECOY,
44. CALLING THE MOOSE,
45. MOONLIGHT ON THE LAKE,
46. INITIAL "A,"
47. SHOEING CANOES,
48. "WOULDN'T TAKE FIFTY DOLLARS FOR IT,"
49. MANSUNGUN DEADWATER,
50. A SKY PICTURE,
51. A TWELVE MILE "DRAG,"
52. FROM THE DRY TO THE WET PROCESS,
53. CAMP ON THE AROOSTOOK RIVER,

ILLUSTRATIONS.

54. INITIAL "W,"
55. A WAITING BREAKFAST,
56. THE FIRST HOUSE ON THE AROOSTOOK RIVER.
57. "CAN YOU GET UP A DINNER FOR THE CROWD?"
58. BIRD-TRAPPING MADE EASY,
59. "SEVENTY SUMMERS,"
60. A PEEP AT THE STRANGERS,
61. PRESQUE ISLE—CIVILIZATION IN FOCUS—
62. VALEDICTORY,
63. FINIS,

INTRODUCTION.

ON page *31* of *Canoe and Camera* I made the following foot-note, in mentioning the fourth tour from Moosehead Lake through the Maine Wilderness: "Still another trip can be made from Churchill Lake through Spider, Echo and Mansungun Lakes to the waters of the Aroostook, leaving the woods at Caribou, Maine. But the scenery is uninteresting, and the difficulties will not compensate one for the labor endured, while woe betide the tourist if the water is low."

I little imagined, as I penned this paragraph from hearsay, that the following season I should so thoroughly acquaint myself with its "difficulties," and learn from actual experience the *beauties* of its scenery.

Yet, in the autumn of 1880, while putting in order

my well-worn camp equipage with no definite plan in view, a letter from my friend and fellow traveller, Colonel G., gave this *fortunate* direction to my fall trip. This letter informed me that the year previous he had discovered a region unknown to the sportsman and tourist, yet accessible by canoe from Moosehead Lake, and was rejoicing in the title of the "Pioneer of the Aroostook." I could not, therefore, be the first to explore this route, and so, accepting second honors, began immediate preparations for the trip.

The oldest inhabitants of Maine *may* have known a drier season than that of 1880, but the reader will perceive in the following pages that a cart, rather than a canoe, might have been used in the exploration of the greater portion of this unknown region.

THE AUTHOR.

HARTFORD, CONN., 1881.

Paddle and Portage.

FROM

MOOSEHEAD LAKE TO THE AROOSTOOK RIVER, MAINE.

ILLUSTRATED AT DAY'S STUDIO, NEW YORK,

FROM

PHOTOGRAPHS MADE BY THE AUTHOR.

CHAPTER I.

"Happy the man who has the town escaped;
To him the whisp'ring trees, the murmuring brooks,
The shining pebbles, preach
Virtue's and wisdom's love."

THE START.—UNWARRANTED ASSUMPTIONS.—OUR GUIDES AND OUTFIT.—A FLIMSY WHARF.—RAILROADING OF THE OLD DAYS.—CONTEMPTIBLE DECEIT TOWARD DUMB ANIMALS.—COMMENCEMENT OF FUN ON THE "CARRIES."—WE GO INTO CAMP.—FIRST NIGHT IN THE WILDS.

O N the 11th of September I landed at the Mount Kineo House, Moosehead Lake, fully equipped for a voyage of over four hundred miles through the wilderness of Maine to New Brunswick. Colonel G., my comrade adventurer, having arrived afew days previous, had engaged the guides, canoes, provisions, and other accessories, so there was little to do save discard the habiliments of civilization.

Two days after, on the morning of the 13th, we started from the Kineo Dock on the little steamer DAY DREAM for the northern extremity of Moosehead Lake, at which point we were to bid adieu to civilization and traverse the remainder of our route alone by paddle and portage.

As the steamer cast loose from the wharf, our interested friends ashore gave us a farewell cheer that echoed across the waters of the lake. In these realms of adventure, everybody is one's friend. Friendship is spontaneous; good feeling reigns supreme, and people that we did not know united with people that we did know in their signal-tokens of "Godspeed"—or, at least, we thought they did. As we passed up the lake, fashionable ladies and gentlemen waved their handkerchiefs upon the piazzas of the hotel.

"This attention is pleasing," remarked the Colonel.

"Pshaw!" I said; "It is warm this morning. Don't you feel the heat of the air? They are fanning themselves."

"Oh!" he said; "I thought they were giving us a farewell."

Down on Kineo pebble beach some of the guides, who hang around the hotel while "open for engagements," were standing in company with a few of the oldest inhabitants, sweeping the air with their broad felt hats in a manner wild and energetic. Pointing these out to me, the Colonel hinted his belief that their actions were intended for us.

"Nonsense," I said; "more likely they're doing battle with a horde of offensive insects."

Not far from this group stood a party of sportsmen, who fired a volley from their rifles that rattled over the lake with a harsh, spasmodic detonation. To me, however, the voice of the report was highly expressive.

"Colonel," I said, with a sudden flush of pleasure; "there's a party of the boys giving us a send-off."

"Fudge," said the Colonel; "do you see that duck flying across the lake? There's the worthy object of the honor. They've missed it. Some bevy of girl-admirers have been watching them from the hotel, and they save their reputation by looking toward us, as if the volley was intended for a salute."

"Oh," I said, collapsing at the Colonel's retaliatory explanation; "I thought it strange that we should cause so much trouble."

In a short while we were ploughing the upper waters of Moosehead Lake, and the frowning bluffs of Mount Kineo began to fade into the distance, the rocks, the trees, and other features of its scenery, becoming indistinct in a haze of deepening purple. As the little steamer moved onward, lying on the deck among the baggage, we took our ease, and listened to the predictions of our few companion-passengers, and studied the glowing eloquence of the cloudless sky, both of which bespoke the ominous fact of the dry season, and told us with cruel blandness to rest while we might, as there was in store plenty of exhilarating exercise upon the "carries" beyond.

While we are progressing to our destination, I will take an opportunity for a description of our guides and general outfit. This some people consider necessary, and it is therefore a duty which sooner or later must be fulfilled.

The guides, for such an extended tour of exploration, had been well chosen. One of them was an Indian, whose tribe had originated on the St. John's River. He lived, however, at Oldtown, Maine. His name was Thomas Nichols. He was a stalwart man, six feet in height, forty-eight years of age, and weighed one hundred and fifty-five pounds. He was considered the best hunter in the vicinity, while his reputation in the manufacture of birch canoes was known throughout the State. He was dressed in a grey shirt, a cardigan jacket, and a black felt hat, which made him look like a savage who had fallen into the clutches of some prowling missionary, and issued from the "conversional brush," not the better of soul, but the richer of a complex and indifferent suit of clothes.

We had two other guides, Hiram and John Mansell, who were brothers from Greenville, Maine, the former officiating as cook, the latter as man of all work. Hiram was clad in a pair of blue pants with red stripes at the sides, a souvenir of military life, and looked like a relic of Bull Run. He wore a jacket of brown duck, with a leather strap about his waist, to which was slung a long bowie-knife, whose sheath was a deer's leg with the hoof attached. He stood five feet five inches in his stockings —how high with his shoes on we are not prepared to

OUR GUIDES.

say—was thirty-one years of age, and weighed just one hundred and forty-eight pounds, before dinner. His brother John, clad throughout in grey woollen attire, was twenty-three years old, but as strong as an ox, and having served a good apprenticeship among the loggers, could wield an axe with powerful effect.

In addition to the provisions necessary to feed five hungry men on a five weeks' cruise, our canoes were further loaded with two canvas A tents, 6 x 8 feet, a Baker tent, 7 x 9 feet, six iron beaver traps, five rubber and canvas bags, containing our blankets, rubber beds, cooking utensils, four Winchester rifles, and a good supply of ammunition.

Last but not least in importance to the expedition was a Tourograph, an instrument with which to photograph the scenery along the route. This apparatus, which was always placed at the head of my tent, was tended with zealous care from first to last, and many were the cautions given the guides as to its disposition in the canoe or on the carries.

"All ashore!" cried Colonel G., as we reached the ricketty wharf at the extremity of Moosehead Lake. This wharf was a sadly dilapidated affair. As we stepped upon it to transfer our baggage to the shore it squeaked like a box of compressed guinea-pigs, and bounced and rocked so beneath our weight that the Colonel declared it had at one time been an Indian baby-charmer.

Gaining land we strapped our canoes and baggage upon a wagon which was in waiting, to which were attached a pair of horses, that were also in waiting, with their goodly snouts immersed in the contents of a monster bag and snuffing after a handful of oats that had been lost somewhere in the interior. Then, as our party gave the steamer a farewell cheer, the Colonel and I led the advance along the sandy path of the North East Carry, leaving the guides to bring up the rear, to prevent any loss of the "kit." As we trudged along, looking to the right, our attention was attracted to an old road along which ran in dubious parallel two long rows of disjointed logs, which were soon lost to sight in the choking wild-growth. These logs had once served as the tracks of a wooden railroad, extending two miles across the fields, over which the loggers, in former years, had drawn their supplies to the Penobscot waters, with the motor power of *oxen*. Theodore Winthrop wrote, that "whenever the engine-driver stopped to pick a huckleberry, the train, self-braking, stopped also, and the engine, or '*bullgine*,' took in fuel from the tall grass that grew between the sleepers." But few traces of these rails now remain, and horse-power has been substituted for that of the more patient ox.

As the Colonel and I progressed, we became quite absorbed in commenting on the features of the route over which we had both travelled so frequently. The sun shone brightly, the birds were twittering merrily on the twigs at the side of the path, insects and other nondescripts buzzed, chirped, hummed, and squeaked with ready avail of the true American privilege of free speech; but so concerned were we in our talk that we failed to notice for some time that there was room enough in the air for other music, which we did not hear. In fact, we missed the sonorous jolt and rumble of the wagon-wheels behind us. Looking back, to our surprise, we found that the vehicle was not in sight.

"A break-down," I suggested; "let us go back and see what has happened."

Retracing our way, in a few moments we came in sight of the wagon. It was standing stock-still in the road. As we ran up beside it, we found our caravan in a most distressing situation. The horses were standing before the clumsy wagon as motionless as statues, and with forward-pricked ears and firmly planted feet were stubbornly refusing to move a step, while the driver and our guides were dancing around them with the grace of frantic Zulus, inciting them to energy with the aid of sticks snatched from the roadside.

"What's the matter?" we inquired.

"Can't git the 'tarnal brutes to budge a step," cried Hiram, desisting from the chastisement, and dropping his stick upon the road in sheer exhaustion.

"What's the reason you can't? Let me get at them!" cried the Colonel, furiously.

"Don't, Colonel," I pleaded, as my comrade began to pirouette in the Zulu dance with flourished stick. "There's no telling what is the cause of their inability. Perhaps the poor creatures have corns."

"No, they 'avent; no sir-ee!" cried the driver, meeting my remark with a howl of indignation. "Nary a spavin, a heave, nur a corn abeout them ar hosses, I'd hev ye know. Finest breed that was ever raised in Maine; they cum all the way from Californy."

"Then why don't they stir their stumps?" demanded one of the guides in a voice that made the animals quiver.

"No cross-questioning. At them again with the sticks, boys!" cried the Colonel. "We'll put life into them."

"No, no ye can't. Thar's only one thing kin inspire them ar hosses."

"What's that?" I asked, breathlessly.

"Oats," replied the driver, mournfully.

"Then where are the oats? Bring out the oats!" cried the Colonel.

"Aint got none. They've all giv out."

"Then where's the bag," I cried, with a desperate idea. "Give me the bag, and I'll start them."

The driver threw me the big oat bag from the interior of the wagon. It fell into my arms like a collapsed balloon. Taking a position in front of the horses, I held it at arm's length toward their noses.

"Now," I cried to the guides; "get behind the wagon

and *push*. Between two fires the engine cannot fail to move."

"You're mad! Tom," cried the Colonel, with a look of supreme disgust.

"Never mind," said I; "there's method in my madness, as you'll soon see;" and he did see, for the next moment the horses, sniffing the oat bags, sprang forward with a desperate spurt after me. All the way along the road, I held the oat bag dancing before their eyes like an *ignus fatuus*. At times, however, the animals half suspected the deceit, and seemed inclined to lose faith in the feeling of man and lag. This made our progress rather spasmodic; but they were never suffered to come to a halt, for at every threatened relapse the guides stood ready to do propeller-power behind.

"This is Rapid Transit with a vengeance," cried the Colonel, as he strode after us convulsed with laughter.

We travelled in this way for some time, until we reached the West Branch of the Penobscot, where the driver and his dashing equipage were cheerfully dismissed and we took to the water in our canoes. Thus the last link between us and civilization was broken. The water was very low, and we found ourselves ushered into a difficult passage. This was the dryest season experienced in Maine for many years.

The water courses displayed such masses of huge rocks and uncovered stretches of gravel beds that, at a distance, one would have thought them logging roads rather than the beds of large rivers. Constantly we were obliged to step overboard and lift our canoes over obstructions, and often we sighed for the aid of horseflesh, of better calibre, however, than that we had just parted with.

After two hours of alternate dragging and paddling we shot into the right bank of the river, and made our first camp half a mile above Moosehorn Stream. Then

"There was hurrying to and fro;"

the baggage was thrown out of the canoes, the latter

were drawn up on the bank and overturned to dry; the tents were unrolled, the poles were struck, and two of the guides busied themselves in their erection, while John Mansell woke the echoes of the woods with the resounding blows of his heavy axe as he cut the logs and fuel for the camp fire, and the Colonel and I, seizing our rifles, sauntered forth with sanguinary strides to decrease the population of the forest game in the interest of our first meal. When we returned we found everything under way; the log fire was crackling merrily, before which were squatted the guides on upturned pails. Around them was scattered in picturesque confusion our full culinary paraphernalia, consisting of tea and coffee-pots, kettles, frying-pans, tin cups, bakers, broilers, etc., out of which assortment they were selecting the utensils needed for our meal. They looked like a band of itinerant tinkers.

Tossing Hiram a brace of partridges the Colonel and I, arranging the Tourograph apparatus, obtained a photograph of our first camp. Soon after that supper was announced, after which sleeping accommodations engaged our attention. Going toward our tent we found that

THE FIRST CAMP.

Nichols, the Indian, had carpetted it as well as those of the guides with fragrant boughs of hemlock. But our two large rubber beds yet remained to be inflated. The size of these were 36 x 80 inches. The Colonel and I began to devise a plan for swelling them without taxing our physical resources. We soon agreed that the only way out of the difficulty was the arrangement of a match on time between two of the guides. Hiram and the Indian seized upon our proposition instantly, and their rival wind powers

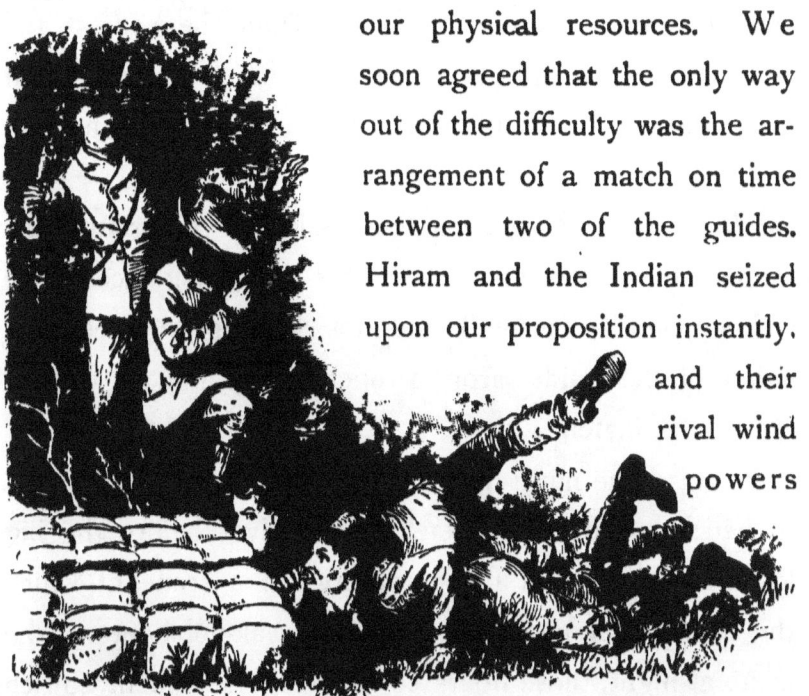

THE BEST MAN TO WIN.

were soon tested. Stretching the collapsed rubber bags side by side, they spread themselves flat upon the

the ground in similar positions, and placing their mouths at the apertures received the signal, and began to blow as if for dear life. The Colonel and I held our timepieces in our hands, and watched the struggle with amusement. They had both powerful lungs and the bags were soon inflated. As they withdrew from the contest, the veins swelled upon their foreheads like whip-cords, and their fiery red faces glowed with the color of a harvest moon.

"Who wonee?" gasped the Indian, as he passed the sleeve of his grey shirt across his perspiring face. The Colonel and I consulted, and not desiring to discourage either of the guides from a repetition of the act we declared the match a tie.

By this time night had set in. But we did not hasten to bed; no, indeed. Stretching ourselves before the big log fire we revelled in the raptures of a scene of which the tourist can never tire—the last wakeful hours of the camp at night, those hours so rife with merriment, so rich with unbosomed anecdote, when the first story, springing from the innocent seed of palpable truth, becomes a prey to those succeeding ones which bear the hideous stain of doubt. Exaggeration is wonderfully prolific. "India-rubber yarns" are told in endless variety, each one being a super-test of the elasticity of the whole. Then some one falls into the error of telling the truth, and his story is howled at as being weak and unpalatable. Finally some one tells the "whopper" of the evening, which bids defiance to retaliation and sends the party to bed in first-class trim for weird dreams. A bomb-shell of this kind from the Colonel was the cause of our dispersal, and exchanging "good nights" we entered our tents. Then, while the camp fire still burned on, while the bark curled from the trunks of the big birch logs, while the cedar snapped with its merry crackle, while the shadows of the leaping flame and smoke danced fantastically upon the ruddy tent walls—we slept.

CHAPTER II.

*" A band of hunters were we. All day long
Our feet had trail'd the woods."— STREET.*

MOVING ON.—PINE STREAM FALLS.—CHESUNCOOK LAKE AND FARM.—UMBAZOOKUS CARRY.—A DRY GROUND SLEIGHING PARTY.—FURTHER EXPERIENCE WITH THE HORSE.—A GLIMPSE OF DESOLATION.—CHAMBERLIN LAKE.—A VISION.—EAGLE LAKE.—SMITH BROOK.—HAYMOAK FALLS.—TROUT STORIES.

BRIGHT and early the next morning tents were struck, canoes loaded, and soon we were afloat upon the waters of the Penobscot, hoping to reach the mouth of the river by nightfall.

Nightfall?

Perish the fond and audacious expectation. It was

not until four days subsequently, after a running battle with difficulties, that we passed the Pine Stream Falls and entered Chesuncook Lake.

CHESUNCOOK LAKE.

There is a farm upon this lake. It consists of a wilderness of ground, and a collection of rickety sheds, clustered like barnacles to a major "pile," which you suspect to be the homestead.

There is nothing pretentious about the architecture. It is of a rather complex order, and the span of life never seemed to me so short as at the moment I attempted to determine it. Such a view of angles, horizontals, and perpendiculars never before greeted my eyes. It was simply distracting. The designing genius must have suffered with a cast in his eye, or a mind disordered through indigestion.

CHESUNCOOK FARM.

These farm buildings stand alone in a wild, open tract of country. The sight of them strikes you instantly as strange and unaccountable. At first you wonder and half believe yourself in the vicinity of Ararat and a debilitated ark. Then you shudder and give thought to a terrible suspicion—a small-pox hospital, perhaps! Finally, unable to reach a plausible conclusion, you forget you are in Maine, and in generous sympathy with the glory awarded to all the super-dilapidated buildings of the lower states, declare at once that the pile must be the old headquarters of General Washington.

We made a brief stay at this farm, spending most of our time in duck and plover shooting.

We then paddled across the lake and passed up Umbazookus Stream, dragging our canoes most of the way. We landed at a carry on the right bank.

During the previous season, while visiting this region, we had pushed further up the stream to what is known as "Mud Pond Carry," sacking our entire kit to Mud Pond. But a longing for the almighty dollar has since been aroused in the heart of one Smith, who having erected a house and barn a short distance from the landing, now transports the tourist's canoe and supplies six miles to Mud Pond, across Umbazookus Carry.

As we neared the house we fired a gun in signal of our approach, and were met by a man and a boy who rushed forth from the adjoining barn. Then

> A party through the Maine wilds bound
> Cried "Good man, do not tarry;
> But tow us o'er the boggy ground
> Of Umbazookus Carry."*

Whereupon the man and the boy began immediate preparations for the transport.

Hastening to the woods they soon appeared with four bony animals in harness that put one more in mind of the rigging of a clam boat than the trappings of horses. These were attached to two large wooden sleds made of tree branches, upon which were placed our birch canoes, swung by an adjustment of ropes to four stanchions at their sides, while the spaces underneath were occupied by our baggage.

These clumsy vehicles, with their strangely arranged cargo, presented a novel and picturesque sight, which I thought a good subject for the Tourograph, and "photo'd"

---

* Copyrighted 1881.

UMBAZOOKUS STREAM.

before starting. Then, amid the cheering of our guides, the horses were whipped up, and we were soon underway,

PORTAGE.

sliding across the logs, bouncing over the rocks, and pitching along through the mud like a fishing-smack foundering in a storm.

The Colonel and I strode ahead with our guns, securing partridges by the way, closely followed by Hiram's team. Soon we heard a shout, and looking back saw his horses rearing and plunging, and the sled stopped short before a tree.

"What's up?" we cried.

"This left-hand nag here is a Tartar," replied Hiram, as he tugged and jerked at the reins. "I tried to tack and leave that 'ere tree on the starboard quarter, but I'll be blamed if he haint sot me into it all kerchunk on the port bow. Say, gineral!" he yelled, turning ferociously toward Smith; "what's the matter with this here animile of yours?"

"Which one? That one?" asked Smith. "I meant to warn ye consarnin' him. He must be handled mighty gingerly. Takes an ingineer to run him properly."

"Why, for sin's sake?" inquired Hiram.

"He's cross-eyed, an' he allers leans hard toward the west."

"Cross-eyed! Poor crittur," murmured Hiram, sympathetically, as he laid the lash along the animal's ribs. "How'd it happen?"

"Don't know exactly. Born so, I expect; but I heerd say onst that the children o' the people who had 'im afore me dropped a nail into his feed bag. Don't know how true it is."

Hiram struggled desperately with the reins to free the sled, but without success.

To back the craft would have required more than the entire strength of the party, so John Mansell's axe came into play, the tree was felled, and leaping over its stump the sled was soon bounding on.

After three hours of heavy toil for both horses and men, we completed the six miles, and arrived at the uninteresting sheet of water called Mud Pond.

"Jemima!" cried Hiram, as he surveyed the pond and gauged the depth of the water; "how are we going to get across?"

"Have to dig a channel with our paddles," said John.

"Me think so—yes!" ejaculated the Indian, as with a miss-step he almost sank from sight in the mud.

A channel was soon made, canoes repacked, and by dint of hard poling we reached deep water, and paddled for the opposite shore a mile distant.

On arriving the same difficulties which prevented our embarking delayed our landing, and at one time it looked as if each man would make his canoe his camp for the night. But just as the sun set we managed to land, and pitched our tents in the dark.

Mud Pond Stream being almost dry, we were forced

the next morning to carry our canoes and kit almost a mile, depositing them at last in the stream which flows through the moose barren bordering on Chamberlin Lake.

Here we found ourselves in a wild, desolate country. The stream along which we moved ran through an immense tract of bog, which was dotted here and there with old stumps reaching for a quarter of a mile in every direction. This was bounded in the dim distance by a dead wood forest, which enclosed it completely like a *chevaux de frise*. Within this was presented a most lugubrious landscape. It was the picture of a region dead to the world and to itself. The old grey stumps scattered about seemed like storm-beaten tombstones which marked the resting-places of perished souls, and the naked, bleached forms of the trees in the palisade like sentinel skeletons guarding a death ground.

Soon with our three canoes in line we entered the waters of Chamberlin Lake. There we were suddenly startled by hearing a loud splash in the water, and greeted with the vision of an immense bull caribou, which sprang up and instantly disappeared in the woods before we could

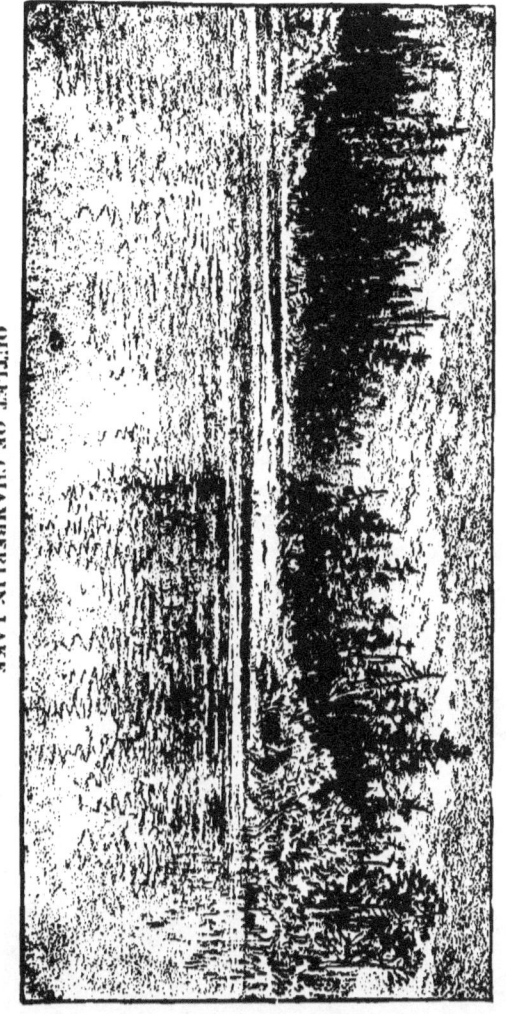

OUTLET OF CHAMBERLIN LAKE.

tender him the slightest compliment at the pleasure of the meeting.

"Confound the luck!" yelled John, throwing aside a rifle in exasperating disappointment.

"Exceedingly impolite of the beast to decamp so suddenly" said the Colonel, as we examined the animal's

CHAMBERLIN FARM.

tracks; "he would have weighed three hundred pounds, if an ounce!"

Chamberlin Lake is eighteen miles long, three miles wide, and is one of the largest bodies of water in Maine. At this point, the preceding year, I turned south through the East Branch of the Penobscot, and landed at Mattawamkeag on the European and North American Railroad. This year our course lay directly to the north.

At Chamberlin Farm we made a brief stay, and

purchased an extra supply of hard tack, sugar, and molasses, as our stores were running short. Then turning our backs on the lovely peaks of Mt. Katahdin and the Soudahaunk range, which lay to the southwest, we buffetted the waves of the lake for six miles, landing at the locks which divide its waters from those of Eagle Lake below.

Here we went into camp, and the Tourograph was brought into important requisition while a benign and smiling sun was at its best. And here we were delayed for three days afterwards, through a go-as-you please rainstorm, during which we tried the camera while the aforesaid benign and smiling sun was at its worst, hid-

FACETIÆ.

HAYMOAK FALLS.

den away like an unfortunate trade-dollar during the storm of repudiation.

When the weather grew favorable, we followed the current of Chamberlin River one mile down to Eagle Lake below.

Some people think of Maine as a state containing only one large lake with an innumerable number of smaller ponds within its borders, but the tourist visiting these regions for the first time is daily surprised by bodies of water which fairly compete with the area of Moosehead. Eagle Lake is thirteen miles long, with an average measurement of three wide. Within its bosom it nurses two islands, while the horizon of its northern extremity is broken by the cone-shaped peak of Soper Mountain.

Our next camp was made at the mouth of a beautiful stream near here, which writhes under the opprobrious title of Smith Brook. This innocent sheet of water, which I am certain has done naught to merit the ignominy it suffers, presents most picturesque beauties in its windings as far as Haymoak Falls.

There we discovered the skull of a large moose, and

extracted the great teeth, fearing they would be the only souvenirs we should obtain of that almost extinct animal.

"My!" said the Colonel, as he pried out one of the grinders; "what a surface for a tooth-ache!"

There, also, we had splendid fishing, and captured many large trout.

The day before we broke up camp we had a run of sport that well-nigh astonished us, and that night at the evening meal we had a rare fish feast, served with the following sauce:

"I don't care whether you believe this yarn I'm goin' to tell ye or not," said Hiram, as he added another vertebra to the pile of trout skeletons accumulating by his plate; "but it's true as gospel, nevertheless an' notwithstanding, an' with me the truth is like the stump of a back tooth—it must cum out. You know, Nichols, where the old farm road from Greenville to Dexter crosses the bridge at Spectacle Pond?"

"Me know," said the Indian, scarcely raising his eyes from the fire.

"Wall, I was guiding for Doctor L. and Squire B. one

day in that region, which happened, by the way, to be a pet fishin' ground o' their'n. As we were gittin' along to the bridge, the Doctor, all of a sudden, says to the Squire, 'If you've no objections, Rufe, I'll slip ahead of you and cast my flies under that bridge, for ten to one I'll strike a big fish, as I saw some mighty fine trout there the other day while crossing to see my patient in the old farm beyond.' The Squire told him to go by all means, but to have some mercy for the sport of other people an' not to altogether clean the brook. With that the Squire turned around, an' began to amuse himself at pistol practice with my old hat that I'd set up for a target on a tree, an' the Doctor, he pegged down the road like mad toward the bridge. I stood an' watched him jest for fun, for he was a comical old duck, an' so nervus an' fussy that I 'spected like's not to see him tumble overboard. Reaching the spot he made a dozen or so wild casts, but at last succeeded in landin' his flies under the bridge, when he took a seat on a projectin' beam, an' let the current sweep 'em out. Quicker'n ye could say Jack Robinson, I heard a shout; the Doctor's rod almost bent double, an' he begun reeling in for dear life. 'I've got him, Mansell; I've got him. Come, quick! he's the biggest fellow I ever hooked.' Grabbin' the landin' net, I ran over the bank to help him. It looked for all the world as if he'd ketched a shark, but as soon as I reached the other side an' saw the game a flappin' on the surface, I give a shout that almost blew me to pieces, an' rollin' down on the bank, I roared until every 'tarnal rib was sore. What d'ye guess had hold of the old fellow's line? Why, nothin' less than a big *Shanghai rooster!* The animile, as I found out after, belonged to the farm near by. It had been hatched and raised with a brood of ducks, an' bein' quite a water-nimp, as they call it, had strolled into the stream to have a pick at the Doctor's flies. I tell ye what, so long as he lives the Doctor'll never forgit that bite, for the shock of the

GOOD SPORT.

discovery knocked him clean off the beam into the water, where I clapped the landin' net on his old bald head an' fished him out like a drowned rat. I don't know how true it is, but they say that ever since he took that bath ther' hain't been another trout seen about the brook."

"Which puts me in mind of another fish story, in which I and an old schoolmaster friend of mine are concerned," said the Colonel, as Hiram concluded. "Out trouting once we suddenly met on our way to the brook a dog, which sneaked out from a patch of woods and began to follow in a close trot at our heels. We were taken somewhat by surprise at his appearance, because of the loneliness of the country, for there was no house within miles of us, and we were puzzled to think where he had come from. He looked the picture of starvation. His skin was literally hanging on him, and the body was so thin and sunken that we almost heard his ribs playing a bone chorus as he jogged behind us. We fed him with a portion of our lunch, which he devoured greedily. Finding himself favored, he followed us to the trouting ground. Spying out a beautiful quiet brook we sat down on the bank and cast our flies. The sport was instantaneous, and for a while continued and exciting, during which time the Professor had the good fortune to capture some half-dozen trout, which equalled in weight and beauty anything I had ever seen. When the luck was on the wane we reeled in our lines, and turned about to gather together our 'catch,' which during the sport we had thrown behind us on the grass. Suddenly the Professor gave a gasp. 'Great heavens!' he cried; 'My half-dozen beauties! Where are they?' We searched the bank, but they could not be found. 'Is it possible that any one is prowling about these parts and has crept behind us and stolen them?' he said. 'I don't think that likely,' I replied. At the same time my attention was attracted to an object lying at the base of a tree. It was our dog—thin, starved and miserable-looking no longer, but swelled out as fat as a potato-bag, and wagging his tail, and smacking his jaws in heavenly transport. 'Professor,' said I; 'look!' 'What! *Another dog!*' gasped the Professor. 'No, the same dog with variations,' I said; 'thanks to the expansive properties of trout, a little rosier in health.' The Professor guessed the truth and gave a groan. He danced about like a lunatic and kicked the dog until it began to snap at his legs. Then with a heavy heart he packed his traps and we left the animal at the tree enjoying its siesta. 'Fate could not harm him—he had dined that day.'"

Rare treats, these fish feasts. Rare tack, these fish stories. But, reader, beware of bones.

CHAPTER III.

> "But who can paint
> Like Nature? Can imagination boast,
> Amid it's gay creation, hues like hers?"—THOMSON.

IN ROUGH WATER.—NORTH TWIN STREAM.—AN INDIAN PADDLE FOR FUTURE USE.—BREEZES, BLANKETS, COLD AND ICE.—SPIDER LAKE.—MANIFOLD CHARMS OF CAMP LIFE.—AT WORK WITH THE TRAPS.—CONCERNING BEAVER.—WE PROCLAIM OUR INTENTIONS.

ARLY on the morning of September 23d we continued down Eagle Lake and through the "Thoroughfare" to Churchill Lake. Then a change came o'er the spirit of the weather. It grew suddenly colder, and as our three canoes prowed into the lake a sharp breeze sprang up which ruffled its usually calm surface into a restless quiver. As the breeze increased to a "blow" the waves were lashed into white caps, and then into billows, until our fragile birch-barks were tossed about like corks.

Each breaker seemed ready to engulf us; but we shipped little water, for the inventive genius of the Colonel had devised a novel covering for the bows of our canoes.

It consisted of a strip of white canvas extending aft about two feet, which was stretched and secured to a brass hoop arched across the canoe, and fastened with brass pins or pegs.

This made the bow of the canoe resemble the fore-part of an immense Chinese shoe. All articles liable to damage by exposure were thus secured from the spray of the waves and passing rain showers. It proved a capital nook for the storage of the camera, guns, ammunition, etc., and was quite a suggestion to Nichols, who was an old canoe maker.

Our course lay through the Eastern arm of Churchill Lake, a distance of only six miles, the larger body of these waters lying to the north, and having for their outlet the Allaguash River.

At one o'clock we beached our canoes and erected our tents at the mouth of North Twin Stream.

As we supped that night on broiled partridge and stewed duck, we little dreamed of the hardships which lay to the eastward, between us and the waters of the great Aroostook River.

Since leaving our camp on Mud Pond Stream, Nichols had been hard at work at odd moments on a long paddle. From a rough maple log-split, it had gradually been shaped into a thing of beauty, and now with pride was being curiously ornamented with all the artistic execution of which the Indian's deft hand was capable.

"Me beat you, boys, when I get to the 'Roostook,'" said Nichols, with a sly twinkle of his eye, as from under his black felt hat he cast a triumphant look at the other guides.

"But perhaps we shall never get there unless it rains," said John.

"Me think so, too," chimed in Hiram, trying to imitate in tone of voice the Indian's favorite expression.

"When the 'Pioneers of the Aroostook' pushed through this country last season," said the Colonel, glancing at me with an air of superiority, "we experienced no difficulty in continuing our voyage one mile above to

A COLD WAVE.

Marsh Pond. On examination, since landing, I find we shall be obliged to 'carry' around the obstructions, and it will detain us a day."

That night we found use for all the spare blankets in camp, and John was repeatedly aroused to replenish the fire.

"What's the matter, Colonel?" I asked, as gazing out from under my warm blankets on the morning of Sept. 24th I discovered my *compagnon-du-voyage* dancing before the fire and rubbing his hands with "invisible soap."

"Well, you just turn out and see. There is half an inch of ice in our camp pails, and a fair chance for skating on the Lake. We shall have to take to snow-shoes, if this weather holds on."

The tents, stiff with frost, were packed in bags, and in "Indian file" at the right of North Twin Stream we started for Marsh Pond, each man burdened to the utmost. Again and again we repeated our trips, between lake and pond, sinking in the mud one instant, slipping on some frosty rock the next, and not until late in the afternoon were our canoes and the last loads of our kit safely landed at Marsh Pond.

Paddling through this water, its name being typical of its character, we ascended a small stream at its head on our way to Spider Lake.

"Me think it getting dark, boys," said the Indian, "and we better make camp at once."

So hauling our canoes on shore we cast about for the most desirable spot.

There was no choice; it was an immense swamp in whatever direction we travelled. We sank almost to our knees in the moss and decayed underbrush. Once the Indian, floundering in the mud with our tent-poles, disappeared completely from sight, and we might have lost him, but the poles sticking up like bare flag-staffs through the dense brush which masked the marsh pools, disclosed the spot where he had sunk from view. When we dragged him out, he looked like a muskrat.

LOW—THE POOR INDIAN.

"Nichols is trying to discover an underground road to the Aroostook," said Hiram. "Guess he's given up all thought o' usin' that long paddle on them 'ere waters."

This place proved the worst camping ground of the whole trip, but despite this fact it had its charms. The tourist soon grows to despise the consideration of personal comfort, when self-sacrifice is required to bring him in direct association with the nature which infatuates him. He becomes like the poet or painter, a creature purely spiritual, who raves in the rapture of exalted soul while his boots ship water by the gallon, while scarcely a rag hangs to his back, and low-dwindling provisions place him on rations intimate with starvation.

DEVELOPING A PLATE.

Thus it was with us. Our surroundings were unpleasant, but apart from this, as we saw them, interestingly picturesque.

TREES PILED ON TREES.

Here we were in the presence of a great dead forest. Across the pools, the rocks, and the brush growth lay the trunks of monster trees prostrated by the winds, storms, and decaying processes of nature. Trees were piled on trees in huge, insurmountable barriers, each one bearing on the other with a crushing force that tore through the limbs and logs, and pressed the massive pile down deep into the soft vegetation of the marsh.

All was grey and lifeless. It seemed as if nature had lain unresurrected since the Deluge, and that the trees had twisted about and embraced each other in their dying agonies. All was dead! dead! dead! The only sign of life upon them was the deep moss that flourished on the decayed and weather-beaten trunks; but this was like the grass above the grave.

The next day for lack of water we dragged our canoes through the remainder of the river to Spider Lake, and camped on a high ledge of rocks on the Southern shore, its dry and picturesque position being in delightful contrast to our last quarters. This lake, three miles long and half a mile wide, set among these forest depths like a jewel in a ring, reflects ten mountain peaks on its surface.

On our way to camp we examined a point of rocks jutting far out into the lake, whose curious construction attracted our attention. It was a perpendicular pile of corrugated stone crowned with a tall growth of spruce trees, which swept like Indian head-plumes to a hill-top beyond.

The rocks at this time arose fifteen feet from the water, but their well-worn sides indicated their covering in any but a dry season. At their base we discovered deep, subterranean cavities, made by the action of the water, and into these with curiosity we pushed our canoes bent on a full investigation. Some were only slight excavations, suggesting the dwelling-places of large trout, or the coverts of the fur animals abounding in the vicinity, but there were others of considerable space, into which we passed without difficulty. Within all was gloomy and damp, and the motion of the water against the cold, slimy walls made a strange phase of music which echoed mournfully through the caverns. They seemed like the abodes of spirits; we could scarcely repress a shudder at the weird effect of the scene.

Many times afterward did we recall with pleasure the

TWILIGHT IN THE WILDS.

delightful experiences of our sojourn at Spider Lake. The charming comforts of a dry and well-pitched camp, the exhilarating sport by the trout pools among the rocks not twenty feet from the tent door, the partridge-shooting in the woods, the ducking on the lake, the adventures of exploration, and the grand scenic surroundings which we still admire in the souvenirs afforded by photography, have made those too fleeting hours "red-letter days" in our memory.

EVACUATION.

"You are not proposing to desert this lovely camp so soon?" I said to the Colonel, as we stood in the tent door gazing out on the lake some days later. It seems a pity after spending so much labor about the camp to leave at once."

"Well, we cannot tarry long; we little know what is

before us if the water courses remain dry; our birch canoes will not endure the strain much longer," was the Colonel's reply. And so we bade farewell to this charming spot.

At night we reached Logan Pond. Before our tents were in position we were overtaken by a drenching rain storm, which we fought through with philosophical patience, hoping it would increase the water along the route. It takes true grit to endure without complaint a rain-storm in the woods, and one must have an abundance of cheerfulness to keep from murmuring.

"You had better set those beaver traps to-night," said the Colonel to the Indian, as he stood drying himself before the fire, and turning about from one side to the other like a roasting turkey.

"Yes, me think so, too," replied Nichols; and suiting the action to the word, he soon started off down the hill with the iron traps over his shoulder, I following him, bent upon investigating all the mysteries of wood-craft.

"You see beaver house over there?" whispered the guide, as we reached a mud dam at the outlet of the lake, at the same time pointing out to me a cone-shaped knob of mud and sticks about ten feet high and six feet in diameter. "One, two, three beaver live there, and me set traps to catch one to-night. Beaver build house with door; then build dam and raise water to cover door to house."

Slipping into the woods the Indian soon returned with a cedar pole ten feet in length and four inches in diameter at the butt. With his axe he split this, and slipping over it the chain ring of the trap, secured it in position by a wedge. The trap was then opened and lowered carefully into the water, and after driving the pole into the mud, the upper end was made fast with twisted grasses to a neighboring tree.

What was our joy on arising the next morning to see Nichols returning from the pond lugging a fine beaver of over forty pounds' weight, held in position on his shoulders by a withe of cedar bark encircling his forehead.

"Me lost another beaver," said the Indian, as he dropped the heavy animal before the tent door for our examination, and wiped the perspiration from his dusky forehead. "Beaver cut pole in pieces and run with trap. Me hunt pond all over, but no find him;" and he displayed as much sorrow over the loss as if it had been a small fortune.

The fur of the animal was in excellent condition. He was three feet in length, with tail 5 x 12 inches, half an inch in thickness, and covered with black, shining scales of leather-like toughness.

"Is there any truth in the story, Nichols, that the beaver uses his tail to build his dam?"

"No! no!" replied the guide, as laying the animal across his lap he commenced to rob him of his "jacket." "No beaver do that. He use tail to make noise to other beavers. It slap on water, make sound like pistol, and give alarm. Beaver push mud and stones from bed of river with front feet to make dam, and when build house walk up straight on hind feet, and hold to breast sticks and stones with front feet. No one hunt beaver who tell such stories."

The animal was soon dressed and stewed for our breakfast. Its taste was similar to that of corn beef, but of a much more delicate flavor, the liver being reserved as a choice dish for the next meal. The tail was one mass of solid fat, which only the Indian, after toasting it before the fire, could digest. The skin was stretched on a hoop four feet in diameter laced with strips of cedar bark, a shingle of wood being used in spreading the skin of the tail.

"Me no like this," said the Indian, arising after the completion of his work. "In my tribe, brave trap beaver; squaw dress him."

"Which is a much superior way," observed the Colonel. "Thus all the world over the gallant brave saddles upon the poor woman the undaintiful share of the work. A great pity, Nichols, that circumstances in your life have abolished the custom, as far as you are concerned."

"Me think so; yes," replied the Indian, with just the faintest idea of what the Colonel meant; and as he turned to wash the grease and blood from his warrior hands he looked the picture of dignity dethroned.

After a few days tarry we pushed on across Logan Pond, made half a mile carry to Beaver Pond, and camped on Osgood Carry at the head of the last water.

"What do you find so interesting?" I inquired of the Colonel, as I saw him examining minutely the side of an old tree not far from the tents.

"Oh! nothing special, except a record I made last year regarding the 'Pioneers of the Aroostook,' which the winter storms have failed to obliterate."

"Then, before we go, we had better leave some relic of this tour," I said.

Accordingly a photographic plate which had been spoiled by sudden contact with the light was drawn from my Tourograph, and scratching the names of the party on its surface, we nailed it to the tree for the benefit of the next comer, adding as a suggestion of our destination "ON TO THE AROOSTOOK!"

CHAPTER IV.

*"The wise and active conquer difficulties
By daring to attempt them: sloth and folly
Shiver and shrink at sight of toil and hazard,
And make the impossibility they fear."*

OSGOOD CARRY.—THE PACK HORSE LEAGUE.—NOVEL TRICK IN PEDESTRIANISM.—CAMP ON ECHO LAKE.—HIRAM TELLS A STORY.—SLUICING A DAM.—MORE CONCERNING BEAVER.—CAMP AT THE MANSUNGUN LAKES.

MAGINE the difficulties we surmounted in our passage across Osgood Carry to Echo Lake.

With the exception of an occasional beaver, duck, partridge, or string of trout captured on the way, we were obliged to carry provisions sufficient for five men, who never failed in their attendance at meals three times a day, and with appetites which only wood life can stimulate.

Add to these provisions the weight of three tents, three blankets for each man, rubber beds, personal baggage, cooking utensils, guns, ammunition, rods, a Tourograph with seventy five glass plates, and three canoes weighing from eighty-five to one hundred pounds each and you have an idea of the toil and hardships of a tramp through this wilderness.

This "Carry" is the water-shed of the St. John's and Aroostook Rivers, and passes over a succession of hills, through swamps, and wind falls.

Although one trip across is but two miles, a return for a second load makes four, and four trips carrying during half the time all one can bear on his shoulders makes sixteen miles, a fair day's tramp in a country where not even a "spotted line" guides the traveler to his destination.

At the time of our appearance there, the ground after the recent rain was in a soft, soggy condition, which made the way slippery and tedious.

As we pushed forward loaded down with our traps,

frequently did a misstep send one of our number "to grass," and smother him among the articles which constituted his burden. Our progress, as Hiram observed, "was slower than cold molasses."

For every step taken forward we slipped two backward, until the idea was suggested to us of turning about and walking in the opposite direction, that we might travel faster.

"Me fix your load for the 'Carry,'" said Nichols to me, as I started off with what I supposed I should be able to transport without halting; "I show you how to fix pack."

Stepping aside into the woods he cut from a cedar broad strips of bark, and passing them about my chest outside of my arms, fastened them to a roll of blankets on my back. On top of this he mounted my Tourograph, and held it in place by another strap across my forehead.

Like a horse being harnessed, I stood motionless, while he placed my rifle on one shoulder, my shot gun on the other, and hung to them an iron tea kettle, cups, and various other cooking utensils.

Everything ready, and having burdened himself with a much heavier load arranged in like manner, we started off up the side of the mountain in search of Echo Lake.

THE PACK HORSE LEAGUE.

It was hard work. Soon I was boiling with perspiration, and the Indian puffing like a grampus. It seemed like a veritable "first of May" in the wilderness.

Occasionally as a fallen log crossed our path we could

AT NIGHT BY THE CAMP-FIRE.

relieve our aching shoulders by resting the load thereon, but never for a moment did we change its position.

Then on we would tramp, over rocks and through the mire, the stillness of the woods unbroken save by the crackle of twigs beneath our footsteps, or the occasional grunt of the Indian guide.

From early dawn until late at night, dividing our party at times into sections, we labored with our baggage, transporting it but half the distance, from whence it was forwarded by a second relay of guides the remainder of the way, and landed in safety at our camp on Echo Lake.

In this vicinity we discovered in the crotch of an aged tree an old folding canvas canoe. This the Colonel, with a burst of delight, recognized as one deserted by the "Pioneers of the Aroostook" in their excursion of the previous year. Running short of provisions they had been forced to abandon it, and make for the settlements as quickly as possible in their other two.

That night about the camp-fire the Colonel told us the story of their privations, and how their final meal consisted of nothing but the boiled bone of a salt ham seasoned with the last crumbs of hard-tack.

This story suggested others of the same kind, and many and interesting were those retailing the experiences of our guides. I give the following, told by Hiram, of the man who was the first to make maps of Moosehead Lake and its vicinity. It gives an idea of the rigors and danger incident to a journey through the woods of Maine in the dead of winter, and may not be uninteresting:

"Ye never heerd me tell about the man who fust tried to make maps o' these 'ere woods, did ye?" said Hiram, as he tossed an extra log upon the fire. "Wall, it's a long story; but I'll try an' load the cart'idge so the bullet won't go far, as I see Nichols a-blinkin' over there like an' owl at high meridian. It was 'long about the Autumn of 1870, if I remember right, that a feller by the name o' Way cum up from down below an' took board in Greenville, foot o' Moosehead Lake. He was quite a spruce lookin' chap for these 'ere regions, an' though still under twenty-one years of age, had seen a deal o' the world in his little day. Wall, Johnny (that was his name,) had come to rough it, an' take his chances for life with the rest of us, though it was said he'd heaps o' money, an' mighty fine fixins' at home; but he was one of them advent'rous splinters as are allers flyin' round

"BY DINT O' PUSHIN' AN' HAULIN'—"

a-wantin' to see more an' more, an' git into wuss an' wuss every step they go. Us boys was mighty busy that year a-loggin', an he enj'yed the fust winter so rattlin' well among us that he cum back the next season. When the snow got good an' deep in Jan'wary, an' snow-shoein' was just fine, we two arranged a huntin' trip an' started out with our rifles an' all the provishuns we could truss on our backs toward Chamberlin Farm. We hunted about there some days, but finally made a hand-sled, strapped our kit on to it, and by dint o' pushin' and haulin' made our way over the fruz surface o' Chamberlin and Eagle Lakes to Smith Brook. Next day we pushed on to Haymoak Brook an' as it cum on to rain we built a hut of bark and camped.

"Johnny was a restless feller, an' fur all tired out with the pull through to camp, thought if we were goin' to stay long and hunt we'd better lay in more provishuns. He was a plucky little feller, too, an' 'though not much used to the woods, could foller a 'spotted line' with the best o' ye. So he made up his mind to switch back to Chamberlin Farm an' git enough provishuns to last out the trip. I thought this a rather crazy freak, for I felt pretty sartin we could manage to pan out with what we had. But Johnny wanted to be sure. Like all city fellers he had a peevish bread-basket, an' fur all he'd spirit enough to rough it in other ways, he couldn't weather the trial of goin' without his straight meal no-how. I did all I could do to hold him back, but it was no use; then I offered to go back with him, but he was bent on doin' the trip alone, an' leavin' me to rest in camp. So, after buryin' his part o' the kit in the snow, he stood ready to start.

"He did'nt want to go back the same way we had come, but had planned to skirt round back o' the lakes, you know—a mighty unsartin kind of bizness, boys, for a feller raised in a hot-house.

"But he plead so hard I finally give in to him, an' with the point o' my ramrod I marked out his course in the wet snow. Says I, 'You see here, Johnny, that mark I jist made goes across Haymoak Lake to Stink Pond. Now don't you forgit it,' says I, 'to keep right on your course to Fourth Lake, for that there line leads into Little Leadbetter Pond, an' by a foot-track, will take ye to Chamberlin Lake, an' then yer all hunk. There's an old log camp on the Leadbetter, right there,' says I, diggin' the rod into the snow. 'Don't go further than that to-night. Camp there, no matter how early ye reach it; lie over till mornin' an then push on.'

"It was the wuss snow shoein' I ever did see, and I ought not to've let the boy go, but I'd said yes, an' I'm not one of them fellers who goes back on his word.

"I buckled on Way's haversack, filled it with graham bread, stuck his hatchet in his belt, slung his rifle over his shoulder, and with many misgivin's saw him disappear in the woods. After he'd left I commenced to get kind o' nervus like, an' wish I hadn't let him go. Afore night I begun to feel terrible skittish about him. I lit my pipe, cleaned my gun, cut boughs and bark from the trees to make our camp more snug, an' tried by fussin' round to git the lad out o' my mind; but 'twant no use —it didn't work wuth a cent. So buryin' the balance of our kit in the snow I started back to Chamberlin Farm by the old path and camped that night on Haymoak Lake, reaching the farm the next night.

"You will bet boys I was scared to find that Way had not got in, but I thought p'raps he was restin' at the old log camp I had pinted out for him on the Leadbetter. John the "toter" came along the next morning from the logging camp—don't you think, he had'nt seen a hair of him either. Wall, the way I got into them snow-shoes was a caution—the deer's hide was gathered over my toes and heels quicker than a trout takes a fly, and I was a-slidin' off into the woods like mad. I kept goin' and goin' hour arter hour, as if the devil hisself was arter me; it was the best time I ever made on snow-shoes, even on a moose track.

"At 2 o'clock I reached Way's camp of the night before, and follerin' his 'sloat' (track) I kept on arter him and in two hours saw him stumblin' along through the snow in front o' me like a lost sheep. I give a shout of joy, and then a wild halloo, as I dashed on arter him. But he plunged on without turnin' a head— he did'nt seem to hear me. I hailed him agin with no better effect, 'Somethin's up. He's not hisself by a long sight,' I said to myself; an' the way I put forrard through that snow would have done honor to a pair o' the seven leagued boots. Jist as I come up with him, an' was about plankin' my paw down on his shoulder, I heerd him give a gasp, an' then he stumbled an' fell in a parfect heap at my feet.

"FOLLERIN HIS SLOAT— HALLOO!"

"'Johnny! Johnny!' says I, 'Brace up. Hiram's here, and yer all safe.' But he was so far gone, he skarce knew me. To his belt was tied a partridge; but this was all the provishuns he had left, an' with his half froze hands he could but jist hang on to his rifle. I took his gun an' haversack, an' goin' before broke down the big drifts with my snow-shoes, an' cleared a track for him to foller. But he was so weak an' benumbed with cold, that every little while he dropped in the snow like a wounded animile, an' begged me to let him alone.

"'Hiram,' he moaned, 'I can go no further. I am so tired. I feel so sleepy. Go on yourself, an' leave me here.' But I warn't a lad o' that kind. I knew pesky well what that there sleepiness meant; it meant nothin' less than a closin' of eyes once an' forever; he would have been cold, stiff, stone dead in half an hour. It didn't take me more'n a brace o' minutes to find a remedy for this. Whippin' out my old knife I cut down a stick from one o' the young trees on the road, an' the way I laid it round that poor feller's body would have been a sight for the chicken-hearted, I tell ye. I beat him like an old carpet until his bones were sore. I fairly warmed him, which was jist what was wanted; an' what with whippin', kickin' him, an' at times cartin' him along on my back, we soon made mile after mile on our way.

"Those were long hours flounderin' on through the snow; but at last we reached Chamberlin Farm, though to tell a gospel truth I felt we never would git in.

"As luck would have it there was a doctor there from East Corinth, an' with his help we were soon at work with snow gittin' the frost out of Johnny's hands an' feet, an' pumpin' life into him. In a week he was up an' about, good as new, an' hunted with us till the followin' April afore goin' out o' the woods.

"As I learned from him arterwards, Johnny had lost his way between Fourth Lake and Leadbetter Pond.

"BEAT HIM LIKE AN OLD CARPET."

The snow there was over three foot deep, an' as the rain had clogged his snow-shoes he turned into an old loggin'-road that he diskivered an' this took the poor feller right smack off his course. He follered the old road till dark, an' not comin' across the old log cabin I told him about, made for the base of a decayed tree, which he reckoned was fifty foot high at the least. This he set fire to, an' sat all night watchin' it burn down. Fallin' asleep towards mornin', when he woke up he found the merk'ry had gone a long way below zero, an' that his feet, though wrapped in four pair o' socks had both frozen. What the poor feller suffered till I found him must have been terrible. Afore leavin' Greenville that Spring, John Way made the fust of a lot o' maps o' Moosehead Lake an' all its surroundin's. Arterwards he jined these all into one, which I used to sell on the boats, and this is the orthority for nearly all the late maps of these 'ere regions."

Beautiful Echo Lake, the head-waters of the Aroostook River, charms one at once by its picturesque location. High mountains encircle it, which make the peculiar

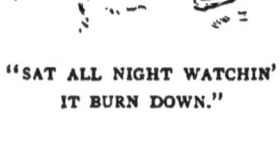

"SAT ALL NIGHT WATCHIN' IT BURN DOWN."

reverberation from which it takes its name, and breathe into the soul that sense of solitude so delightful to the spiritual nature.

We spent three days here hunting and trapping, and added three beaver to our collection of furs and stock of provisions, which latter was now rapidly decreasing.

On breaking camp we explored the outlet of the lake, and, finding the stream very dry, were obliged to build dams in order to sluice our canoes through this country to the Mansungun Lakes below.

"I tell you that water is cold," said John Mansell, as he waded ashore after putting the last mud and stone upon a dam opposite the camp. "You don't call this a canoe tour, do you, Hiram? I should call it going overland to New Brunswick. Never did see such a dry time in my life."

The water having greatly increased during the night, we loaded our canoes and placed them in line above the dam, each man, with the exception of the Colonel, being in his customary position.

"Are you all ready?" yelled the Colonel, standing on the top of the dam below us.

"Ready!" was answered; and with the blade of his paddle he threw the mud and rocks to the right and left, and the pent-up waters of three days' detention swept us down the stream a long way on our voyage. The Col-

BEAVER DAM—FOUR FEET HIGH—ONE HUNDRED FEET WIDE.

onel, dashing through the woods, regained his canoe at a bend in the river.

But gradually the water receded from under our barks, and we were again forced to take to the stream and lift our canoes over the cruel rocks, until we reached a broad expanse of the river below.

This pond was the result of an enormous beaver dam four feet high and one hundred feet wide.

SLUICING A DAM.

"We better set our traps," said Nichols; "many beaver here; me catch some to-night, a family of nine," the Indian's accuracy regarding the points of wood-craft being at times wonderful.

"But we cannot proceed without water," said the Colonel, observing the stream very dry below.

We therefore set our traps and cut the dam to the width of over ten feet, through which the water rushed with velocity, and floated us quickly to the Third Mansungun Lake. We were detained only by a few fallen trees, which the axe in the brawny hands of John Mansell soon cleared.

Before it was light the next morning the Indian's canoe was far away on the lake for an examination of the traps; he soon returned with four immense beavers, whose aggregate weight fell not short of two hundred pounds.

"Me footed two more," said the guide, exhibiting the webbed feet of the animals in corroboration of the fact; "but they very quick—they get away. I see dam we cut last night, and it now just good as new."

"Good as new!" we echoed. "Impossible."

"True as me stand here," said Nichols, at the same time glancing anxiously into the stew pan, to see if we had left him any beaver meat for breakfast. "Beaver, they fell tree in night ten inch thick, gnaw it in lengths three feet long, plant them at cut, and heap with much bark, mud and sticks. Build dam up in one night. No think it myself, if not see it with own eyes. You go see, too."

Astonishing as it may seem, the Indian was perfectly correct in his statement.

After our toil on Osgood Carry and the stream below, we rested over a week on these Mansungun Lakes. The third Mansungun Lake, on which we first camped, is five miles long and two wide. This is connected by a narrow outlet with the second Mansungun Lake, which is about the same size as the other, while the first or lower lake is the smallest body of water, being about two miles long and one wide. I fished and hunted in short excursions from camp, and, with Tourograph over my shoulder, I was constantly in search of the picturesque. Nichols had discovered a brook (the name of which we afterwards learned was Chase,) tumbling down the side of a moun-

CHASE BROOK.

tain near our camp, and as falls were a rarity on the route I spent half a day in this gorge.

About this region we had rare success in our hunting and trapping, and with many skins stretched on the drying hoops about camp, and fresh animals coming in to add to the stock, our quarters gradually assumed the appearance of a Hudson Bay trading-post.

CHAPTER V.

> "'Tis night upon the lake. Our camp is made
> 'Twixt shore and hill beneath the pine trees' shade.
> 'Tis still, and yet what woody noises loom
> Against the background of the silent gloom;
> One well might hear the opening of a flower
> If day were hushed as this."

A VISION ON THE LAKE.—NICHOLS' BIRCH-HORN.—A MIDNIGHT HUNT UNDER A COLD MOON.—CALLING THE MOOSE.

TWO days afterwards the Colonel and Hiram, returning from an excursion down the lake, drew their canoes up on the shore, and entered the camp looking as sorrowful and dejected as a couple of jilted lovers.

"What's the matter?" I asked with alarm, for John Mansell happened to be out also, and the fear struck me at once that something might have happened him.

"Matter? you would not ask it if you had been with us to-day and seen the moose," replied the Colonel sadly.

"MOOSE? YOU DON'T SAY SO! WHEN? WHERE?"

"Moose! you don't say so! when? where?" I exclaimed, and in this frantic query I was joined by the voice of the younger Mansell, who at that moment suddenly appeared behind us from the woods.

The Colonel's voice choked itself in a feeble struggle at reply, and stacking his Winchester against the back of the tent, he threw himself with a disconsolate air down upon his bed. But Hiram, less crushed by the evident misfortune, kindly obliged me with a graphic detail of the trouble.

"It was down on the second Mansungun Lake. We was paddlin' up that stream to the right, where we shot

"OH, SUCH A PAIR OF HORNS!"

the mink yesterday, and the Kernel was whippin' the stream with his fly rod, when all of a sudden we heerd a crackin' of the bushes, and then out on the edge o' the bank stalked one of the biggest bull moose I ever did see. He'd have weighed more'n a thousand pound,

Nichols, sure as I stand here. Oh, *such* a pair of horns!" and the guide's arms were raised in a tremendous gesture.

The Colonel groaned, and raising himself on one hand he swept the other frantically through the air and gave us a magnificent idea of the spread of the horns from tip to tip.

"Then," continued Hiram, "up started the Kernel, and slingin' his rifle to place he pegged in the lead afore ye could count a brace o' winks. Did the bull drop?—no—didn't even give a quiver, for the ball cut wide. Did he turn flanks and tear off—no sir-ee; he waded nearer and nearer to us, till he was only *eight rods off* at the most. 'Pepper him agin, Kernel, and fire low,' I whispered, a-tryin' to steady the canoe. Then bang! went the Kernel agin, an' with a thunderin' snort the bull wheeled 'round, and went smashin' away through the woods."

"An' you missed him clean?" said John.

"No! not the last shot, that hit him somewhere in the neck, for we found his blood on the ground afterwards, but the first ball cut the alders three foot over his head. It was the queerest thing you ever see. Why! I was so sure of him, that I was figurin' how I was goin' to get the carcass back to camp, an' smackin' my lips over the steaks."

"Oh! don't speak of it! don't speak of it! I shall *never* have such a chance again as long as I live; no, never! never!" and the Colonel threw himself back on his blankets with a groan.

I smiled for an instant. I could have "Pinafored" him then and there upon the spot. It was a glorious chance, but his gun was standing close beside him and I did not dare.

"But it's something to have *seen* one, in his native wilds," I remarked, trying my best to comfort him; "the animal will soon be extinct in this country."

It was of no use, and I think that lost opportunity threw a veil of sadness over the Colonel's mind for the remainder of the tour; at any rate, it was a delicate subject to touch upon afterwards.

"If moose so near," said Nichols, one day, "me better make horn and call moose to-night; no try, no get him."

We thought this a good scheme, and with the approval of all the Indian tramped off into the woods, and soon returned with a large piece of birch bark. Shaving the edges with his knife, he warmed it over the fire, and proceeded to roll it up into a great horn two feet in length, tapering it from six inches to one in diameter, and fastening the edges with wooden pegs.

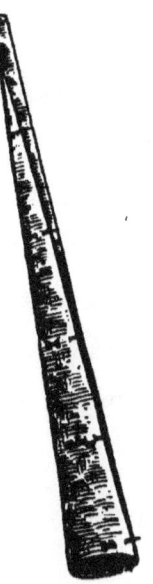

THE DECOY.

Nichols and I were the only ones who went out on the hunt. Preparing ourselves after the evening repast, we stepped into our canoes at 7.30 o'clock. It was not a remarkably severe night, but as I knew I should be obliged to remain for a long time in almost motionless position, I took precautions to wrap up extremely well, and before I returned, the night chill had penetrated through it all to the very vicinity of my bones.

"Most ready?" asked the Indian, as in this clumsy and uncomfortable attire I rolled, rather than seated, myself in the bottom of the canoe.

"Yes; all ready, Nichols!" and throwing the birch moose horn into the craft we paddled out into the lake, with the best wishes of the rest of the party from the shore.

"If we hear a shot," yelled the Colonel, with a look of dubiousness, "we will add an extra log to the fire."

"And cut up the balance of our salt pork," added Hiram, "for moose steak is a little dry without it."

It was a clear night, and so still that the sound of voices and the blows of an axe at camp could be easily heard two miles across the lake. The bright October moon was gradually creeping down the western sky, but shone enough to light us on our way many miles.

> "She shone upon the lake
> That lay one smooth expanse of silver light;
> She shone upon the hills and rocks, and cast
> Within their hollows and their hidden glens
> A blacker depth of shade."

The tall hemlocks that fringed the shore threw their shadows far out into the lake, and in these reflections the guide paddled from point to point.

A slight rustle behind me and the Indian draws forth the long birch horn, dips it noiselessly in the water, and for the first time in my existence I listen to the weird sound of the moose call.

CALLING THE MOOSE.

Ugh—ugh—ugh—oo—oo—oo—oo—oo—ugh—ugh!

Three plaintive "ughs," then a prolonged bellow, commencing in a low tone, increasing in power and volume to the end, and followed by two notes like the first.

It rolled across the lake in every direction, was tossed from mountain tops to the inmost depths of the forests, echoing and re-echoing. Then all was hushed, and we waited in silence the result. The stillness was something overpowering. We held our breaths. At times, however, it was harshly broken. Away toward the distant shore some sportive animal would splash in his gambols at the water's edge, or a musk-rat could be distinctly heard gathering his evening meal; then the prow of the canoe would graze the rushes or the lily-pads with a suddenness that was startling.

Noiselessly the Indian plied his paddle, and we crept silently on in the shadows. Again the horn was raised to his lips, and there came forth that strange midnight call so melodious to my ears. This was repeated again and again for six successive hours, neither of us exchanging a word during the entire time.

At last the stars alone cast their reflections in the

glassy lake, and although from a distant mountain side we at last received an answer to our call, we could not draw the animal to the water's edge.

We had paddled over ten miles. It was now 2 o'clock in the morning, and we returned to camp. I was too stiff to move, and the Indian lifted me from the canoe to the shore, while I realized that I had experienced all the pleasures of moose hunting—save the moose.

CHAPTER VI.

*"And now the thicken'd sky
Like a dark ceiling stood; down rushed the rain
Impetuous."*—MILTON.

DECREASE OF OUR PROVISIONS.—FACE TO FACE WITH STARVATION.—SORE TRIALS.—SHOEING CANOES.—THROUGH THE STORM.—WE SIGHT THE WATERS OF THE AROOSTOOK.—"HURRAH!"

AFTER this adventure we moved our camp to the foot of the first Mansungun Lake, which has for its outlet a river bearing the same name.

After arranging our camp we sent the guides ahead to explore the country in our advance, and ascertain the pitch of water in Mansungun Stream.

"There's more work ahead," said Hiram, in a disconsolate tone of voice on returning to camp, "The water's jest about deep enough to float a turtle. We're in for a long 'drag,' an' I'm afeard our canoes won't never reach the 'Roostook waters unless somethin's done to pertect 'em."

A council was held, and at the suggestion of Nichols, we at last decided to build sleds or "shoes" for our canoes, and drag them through the bed of the stream twelve miles to the Aroostook River.

Little by little our provisions had given out. First the sugar, then the hard tack and coffee, while potatoes and Indian meal had been a thing of the past for many days. The trout had left the summer pools for their spawning beds, and notwithstanding the state of our larder, we had no time to ascertain their whereabouts.

Occasionally we shot a duck or partridge; we added plenty of water to the stew, to make sufficient for the party, and in consequence had an unsubstantial meal.

For many weeks we had subsisted almost entirely on the flesh of beavers, but now being in haste we had little time to set our traps.

On the 20th of October starvation almost stared us in

SHOEING CANOES.

the face. Our breakfast this day consisted of the last portion of beaver flesh and a cup of tea without milk or sugar.

"I believe I'd give ten dollars a mouthful for another

"—WOULDN'T TAKE FIFTY DOLLARS FOR IT."

meal like that, 'though its only an appetiser," said Hiram, arising from the frugal repast.

"Hiram," remarked the Colonel, "puts me in mind of an Englishman I met some weeks ago at the Tremont Hotel, Boston. The gentleman sat at my table, and for four mornings in succession I had noticed him call for dried herrings and coffee, of which he made his entire meal. I was wonderfully interested, and on the fifth morning, to satisfy my curiosity, I had the audacity to question him; 'I say, my friend, you must excuse me; but do you eat those herrings from a medicinal motive, or because you really love them?' 'Well,' he answered, with a drawl, 'I don't exactly *love* them, but along about 11 o'clock in the morning there creeps over me such a glorious thirst that I wouldn't take fifty dollars for it!'"

But this was no time for story telling, and we immediately set to work on the "shoes" for the canoes.

The guides soon felled a number of tall cedars and dragged them into camp.

Then we split them into boards ten feet in length, half an inch in thickness, and tapering from four to two inches in width, the broadest extremities lapping one another at midships.

Sixteen of these strips were necessary for each of the three canoes, and were fastened to their bottoms by being split at the edges and drawn tightly together with strips of cedar bark which ran through the slits, and passing upward were tied securely to the thwarts. Thus the

MANSUNGUN DEAD-WATER.

graceful form of the birch was lost in the rough outline of a boat.

For four days we labored incessantly at our task, and from the splitting of the great logs to the finishing of the wood had as tools only an axe and a penknife. Fortunately partridges proved abundant, and on these we subsisted during our forced encampment. A fine otter four feet in length was shot near camp, but his flesh proved too fishy for us, half-famished as we were. A large hawk frightened by our voices, dropped from his talons a trout of over two pounds in weight, suggesting to our minds Israelitish experience.

A SKY PICTURE.

Among all trying circumstances we kept at work, and

cheered one another by incessant jokes on the situations.

At last the "shoeing" of the canoes was accomplished, and repacking our luggage, we paddled down the dead water of Mansungun Stream, and passed falls five miles below.

Although the morning was lowery, we little thought we had selected the worst day of the entire tour for the passage of the river; but so it proved.

Soon the heavens grew dark, the birds sought shelter in the wooded depths, the wind howled among the tall forest trees, and the rain, beginning first with light showers, increased at last in volume to a perfect deluge.

In the midst of this we were obliged to disembark from our canoes and drag them through the rocky bed of the river, and the good results of the "shoeing" at once became manifest.

"You look out for the bow, me look out for stern," yelled Nichols, as crowding my canoe forward over the ledges of rocks and through the shallow water of the stream we pushed onward, followed by the remainder of the party.

A TWELVE MILE DRAG.

We soon realized that we were in for hard work.

Mile after mile we dragged the canoes, at one moment plunging into some unseen hole almost to our waists, the next instant striking a ledge with hardly sufficient water to cover our feet, while the rain poured in torrents upon us. It was water above and water below, and when we were thoroughly wet, it made little difference from which source it came.

Occasionally we reached water sufficiently deep to float us a short distance, but after a few trials we found it less fatiguing to remain in the stream all the time.

I pulled and hauled until every muscle seemed strung to the tension of a fiddle-string, and before the end of the ordeal I felt like a beast of burden.

So did the others; but we never grumbled. A common feeling inspired us with the idea that it was heroic sport.

After nine hours of toil and discomfort, through difficulties that lasted for twelve miles, we reached the mouth of the stream, and camped at the junction of the Mansungun and Millnoket Rivers, our hardships forgotten in the first sight of the Aroostook waters.

But for the cedar splits protecting the canoes, they would hardly have withstood this rough experience, as the knife-like rocks had left deep impressions on them.

Our rubber bags had shielded our tents and blankets, from the ill effects of the storm, but the Tourograph had been floating unobserved in two inches of water, which destroyed a number of the plates, changing them from the "dry" to the "wet process" of photography.

IN CAMP ON THE AROOSTOOK RIVER.

CHAPTER VII.

> " Now, my co-mates, and brothers in exile,
> Hath not old custom made this life more sweet
> Than that of painted pomp? are not these woods
> More free from peril than the envious court?"

REDEEMED FROM STARVATION.—THE FIRST HABITATION ON THE AROOSTOOK.—MR. BOTTING'S HOUSE.—THE TOUROGRAPH ASTONISHES THE NATIVES.—PURCHASING SUPPLIES AT MASARDIS.—HOMEWARD BOUND.—AU REVOIR!

HEN I turned out the next morning the first thing I heard was an exclamation from the Colonel.

"What a jolly place for trout!"

"Trout!" we echoed. "You don't mean it?"

"I do, every time, my hearties," responded the Colonel, as he cast his line far out on the surface of a dark foam-flecked pool at the junction of the two rivers. The next instant we saw his rod bend like a whip-lash, and as

the speckled prize which weighed above two pounds shot up out of the stream, five hun-

A WAITING BREAKFAST.

gry men fastened their eyes on it with ravenous fascination, and smacked their jaws in anticipation of a breakfast.

"Bravo, Colonel! Do it again!" we cried, as the trout was landed; and verily he did it again and again, while we did them all to a brown in the frying-pan.

During a few days rest here we secured a number of views, hunted partridges, and captured four fine beaver. Aside from the value of the pelts of the latter animals, they placed us once more beyond the chance of starvation; and having lived for a month almost entirely on their flesh, we had learned by experience that it was better than nothing.

We still retained the "shoes" on our canoes, for although each day the Aroostook River grew deeper and wider, we were obliged to repeat the experiences of Mansungun Stream.

On we paddled, day after day. Soon we passed the junction of the Mooseleuk and Aroostook Rivers, and great was our joy when at last we caught sight of the first house since leaving Chamberlin Lake.

From an architectural point of view it would hardly have interested the humblest carpenter, but to our longing eyes it was the assurance of perils over and the hardest part of the tour accomplished.

A rough log cabin, with barn adjoining, and a few acres of cleared land constituted the farm of one Philip Painter. Here, as I was focussing the camera for a picture, a mother and three children gazed on me from the window, and viewed my operations with astonishment.

THE FIRST HOUSE ON THE AROOS'OOK RIVER.

But being still over one hundred miles from the end of our voyage, the tarry was of short duration.

The Colonel, however, in prowling about the farm, found time to fill his pockets with a quantity of small apples, no larger than nutmegs, and about as digestible. He distributed them among the party as we were returning to the boats, imagining that he had made a glorious capture.

"Splendid, aren't they?" he said, as we began to munch them.

"Anything for a change from beaver stews," I replied. "I feel that I could take to boot-leg cheerfully."

A mile further on another farm appeared, perched upon a high bluff.

"We must take this place by storm!" cried the Colonel. "We must find a straight North American meal if we perish in the attempt," and he led a gallant advance toward the farm house.

Mr. Botting, the proprietor of the place, appeared in answer to our hail and greeted us with a stare of open-eyed wonder. The first words he spoke were in company with a jerking action of his thumb toward the Tourograph.

"What kind of a machine do ye call that?" he asked, eyeing the instrument with a profound glance.

"This," said the Colonel, hastening to explain, "is the improved Gatling gun."

"An' ye've come all the way to this God-forsaken hole to sell it?" said the man. "What's it fur, anyhow?"

"Cats," replied the Colonel, with the gravest expression in the world.

"Wal, we ain't got no cats round here," said the man. "Haint seen the ghost o' one in years."

"Don't believe him," I said, interposing. "It's not a Gatling gun; it is a camera—an instrument for taking pictures—likenesses."

"Oh!" drawled the man, "I see! He–he! Queer lookin' affair, ain't it? Looks like one o' these patent coffee-grinders I seed down at 'Guster (Augusta) when I was there last."

"Sir, you insinuate," said the Colonel. "We have had neither sight nor taste of coffee in weeks, and we don't sport a coffee-grinder for bare admiration's sake, we can tell you."

"Which brings us to our business," said I. "We have just come from Moosehead Lake. Can you get up a dinner for the crowd?"

"Wal, yes, I guess so," said the man in a half-dubious tone, as he took in the calibre of the party.

Then, beckoning us to follow, he hobbled back into the house, where after an hour's tarry we were served with a dinner that hardly paid for the time lost in eating it. It consisted of bread, potatoes, and tea sweetened with molasses; but, like the apples, even this was "a change" from beaver stews.

"Must a-had a dry time, gen'lmen,"

"CAN YOU GET UP A DINNER FOR THE CROWD?"

he said, as he busied himself attending to us. "Didn't find much water, I guess. Never did see the 'Roostook run down so low in all my life, an' I've lived on this 'ere river now nigh on thirty-seven year. I'm seventy odd year old, but only for a lame hip I've got I could tramp through the woods with the best o' ye."

"You must have some trouble in working your farm," remarked the Colonel, surveying the fields in front of the door.

"Oh, no; not much. I raise sons to do it. I've got eleven as likely boys as you ever did see; but I lost one in the war—poor feller!" as in a husky tone of voice he pointed to a framed certificate of his son's war services.

Sixteen miles more of vigorous paddling brought us to the town of Masardis, the post-office of the county, and landing on the shore among a number of dug-outs and batteaux, we entered the village.

"Where is the store?" inquired the Colonel, as he crossed the street and rapped at the door of one of the houses.

"Don't have any," said the lady who answered his call, surprised at her visitor.

"Well, can you sell us some flour, potatoes and coffee?" and then the Colonel unrolled his memorandum of much needed camp supplies.

At this house we purchased flour, at another potatoes, at another coffee, no two articles being had at the same place, while chickens at twenty-five cents each were sold "on the run," the Colonel and Hiram securing them after an energetic race.

BIRD TRAPPING MADE EASY.

An old lady of seventy summers, who sold me a box of honey and was very communicative, said during a short but delightful conversation—"I suppose you have heaps more people down in Connecticut than we have in this town; but I don't believe they are half so happy as our townsfolks. Oh, no! they can't be near so happy

—except, well—except on election days;" and a sad expression came over her wrinkled countenance, for the smaller the town, the greater is the feeling on politics in Maine.

"SEVENTY SUMMERS."

The river now widens to a distance of over one hundred and fifty feet, and day after day shows a gradual increase in its depth and power.

The current sweeps us swiftly onward through rapids innumerable in the full excitement of canoe life, but occasionally we are forced to disembark and drag our canoes over a rocky beach, which obliges us to retain the "shoes."

At our various camps we are visited by the inhabitants along the route, who in return for the history of our tour entertain us with news of the outside world, from which we have been separated for so many weeks. Then we begin to realize that we are homeward bound.

An invitation to one of these callers, requesting the

honor of his company at breakfast was accepted (with avidity), although, as he remarked, "the old woman was waiting to serve that meal for him on yonder hill."

A PEEP AT THE STRANGERS.

On passing the towns of Ashland and Washburn, the foamy and discolored appearance of the stream gave evidence of the potato starch manufactories in the vicinity.

The strangest peculiarity of the inhabitants was their utter ignorance of the country and its surroundings.

These people, living on the river, could not give us the faintest idea of distances to points along the shore.

"Hello, stranger!" yelled the Colonel, as rounding a bend in the stream he spied a man standing in one of the log-houses that dot the banks; "can you tell us how far it is to the next town?"

"Dunno, friend; but its nigh on ten miles by the road."

Another gave the same answer, while a third did not know the name of the next town, although he had lived five years in the country—a parallel to the Virginian woodsman who stalked forth from his native pines one day to learn that there had been such a catastrophe in the history of his country as the war of the Rebellion

"Wake up, boys," yelled the Colonel, arousing the party (4 A. M.) at our last camp near Washburn, where we turned out in the dark to partake of a hasty breakfast before embarking.

"If we are going to make forty-five miles to Caribou to day, we must make hay while the sun shines,—or

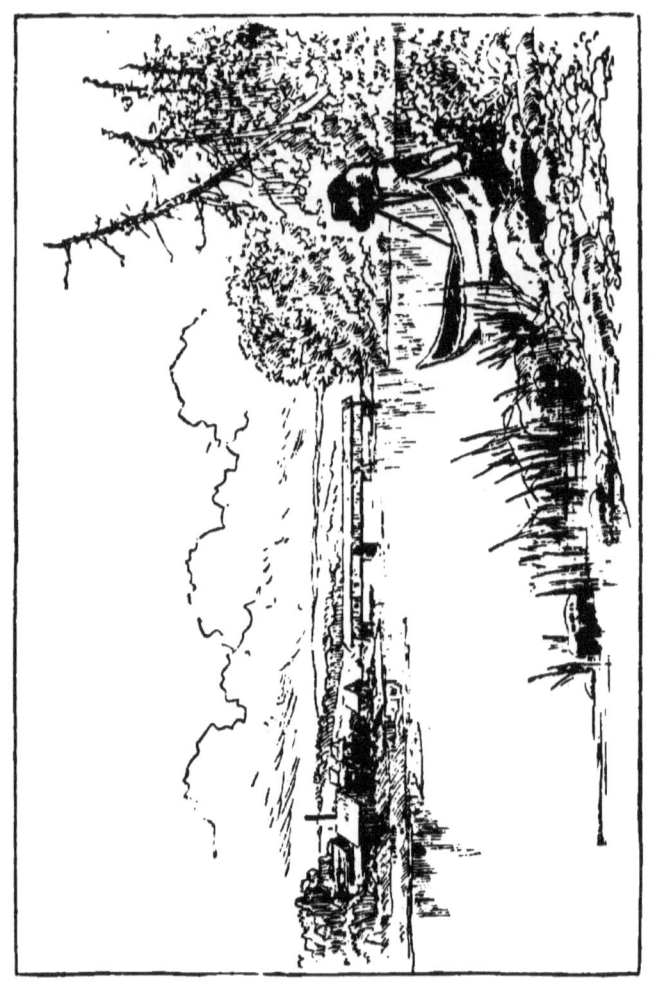

PRESQUE ISLE.—CIVILIZATION IN FOCUS.

while it doesn't shine," he added, as he took notice of the darkness.

Soon we were gliding down the swift stream, avoiding the huge rocks dimly appearing through the mist, until at last the rising sun dispelled the darkness.

At Presque Isle we landed, and while the guides were preparing dinner, I climbed a neighboring hill with my Tourograph and secured a picture of the scene.

Hour after hour we labored at the paddles, until they seemed almost a part of ourselves; the "shoes" on our canoes retarded us not a little.

The sun was creeping down the western sky, and the tall pines on the bluffs above us threw their lengthening shadows across the stream, as doubling the last bend we shot the canoes along side the wharf at Caribou, and completed our tour of over four hundred miles from Moosehead Lake to the Aroostook River.

Here we took the cars.*

---

* Since this canoe tour was completed the railroad has been extended to the town of Presque Isle, at which point tourists can leave the Aroostook River, saving themselves a tedious paddle of about twenty-two miles to Caribou.

A delegation of the "big people" of the vicinity saw us off.

VALEDICTORY.

At the parting moment they seemed visibly affected, as our sketch shows.

As we crossed the line at Fort Fairfield the following day on our way to Woodstock, New Brunswick, the custom house officer found nothing in our kit to reward his examination, although he displayed much curiosity in the leather case containing the camera.

"You must have had a fine time," he remarked.

"Yes," was the reply, "save building dams and shoeing canoes."

While the Indian ejaculated—

"Me think so, too; yes!"

In the whirl of the outside world the weeks fleet by as with the swiftness of a day, but in the solitude of the wilds it seems a longer lease of time.

It is like an age since we took leave of civilization and plunged into the heart of the forests. Now, out of the depths, with a bound we are again in the noise of the busy world.

Mighty trees, primeval rocks with draperies of vine and moss and lichen, tumbling cascades, rushing streams, and all the forest's wealth of color, form and music disappear like magic.

Presto! what a change!

From the sigh and rustle of the grand old pines list to the rattle of rail cars, the shriek of whistles, and hum of machinery in the mills and factories.

From the croon of the night-bird, that with the distant star has often been my only company in the dark hours while my comrades slept, list to the bark of dogs and crow of cocks, as we rush past town and hamlet through the night and early morn. We are out of the wilds. Farewell, Nature! Welcome, Home!

> "There is a pleasure in the pathless wood,
> There is a rapture on the lonely shore,
> There is society where none intrude—
> * * * * * * *
>
> To sit on rocks, to muse o'er flood and fell,
> To slowly trace the forest's shady scene,
> Where things that own not man's dominion dwell,
> And mortal foot hath ne'er or rarely been;
> To climb the trackless mountain all unseen,
> * * * * * * *
>
> Alone o'er steep and foaming falls to lean—
> This is not solitude; 'tis but to hold
> Converse with Nature's charms and view her stores unrolled."

www.ingramcontent.com/pod-product-compliance
Lightning Source LLC
Chambersburg PA
CBHW030350170426
43202CB00010B/1319